NERVES TO SENSES

Design	David West Children's Book Design
Editorial Planning	Clark Robinson Limited
Picture Researcher	Emma Krikler
Illustrator	Aziz Khan
Consultant	Dr Stuart Milligan Physiologist

© Aladdin Books 1991
Designed and produced by
Aladdin Books Ltd
28 Percy Street
London W1P 9FF

First published in
Great Britain in 1991 by
Franklin Watts Ltd
96 Leonard Street
London EC2A 4RH

ISBN 0-7496-0536-7

A CIP catalogue record for this book is available from the British Library.

All rights reserved

Printed in Belgium

HANDS·ON·SCIENCE

NERVES TO SENSES

Steve Parker

GLOUCESTER PRESS
London · New York · Toronto · Sydney

CONTENTS

NERVES	6
THE NERVOUS SYSTEM	8
THE BRAIN	10
PERCEPTION	12
MEMORY	14
NERVES TO MUSCLES	16
SEEING	18
HEARING	20
SMELL	22
TASTE	24
TOUCH	26
INTERNAL SENSES	28
EXTRAORDINARY SENSES	30
GLOSSARY	31
INDEX	32

This book is about the nerves that carry messages around the body, the sense organs that give information to the nerves, and how this information is interpreted and used. The book mainly describes the human nervous system, but also tells you about other animals. There are "hands on" projects for you to try, and "did you know?" panels of information for fun.

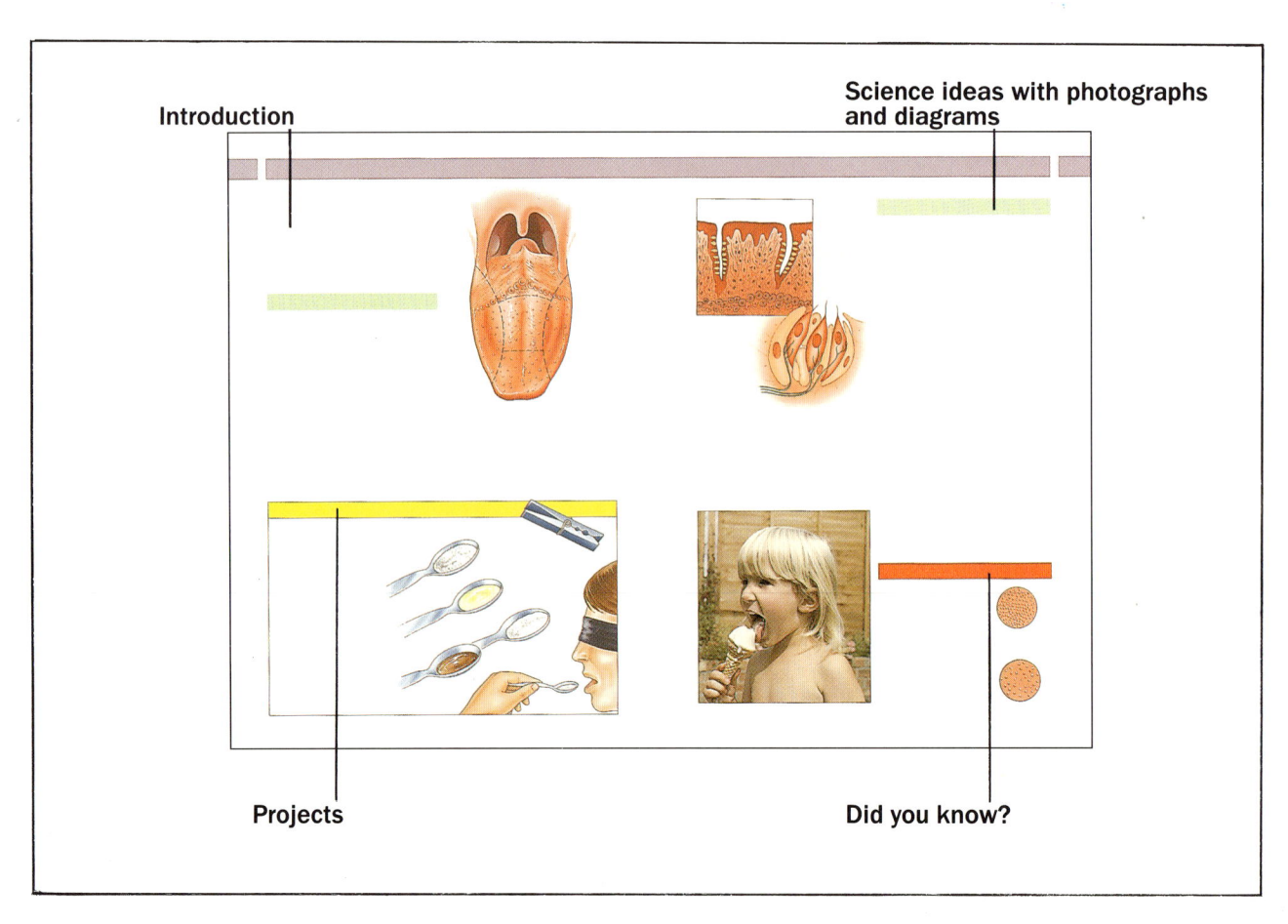

Introduction

Science ideas with photographs and diagrams

Projects

Did you know?

INTRODUCTION

Most types of animal have nerves. Even very simple animals like jellyfish have a basic nervous system. Nerves are the quickest way to send information and instructions around the body of an animal.

The nervous system of humans is perhaps the thing about us that is most different from other animals. Our ability to think using the brain (which is part of the nervous system) and our skill with our hands (which are controlled by nerves) have shaped the world we live in.

This book describes the human nervous system, and also mentions birds, other mammals and reptiles. But the nervous systems of other animals basically work in the same way as the human system. The biggest difference is usually that their central nervous system, especially the brain, is very much simpler. Sometimes — for example, in jellyfish — there is no brain at all.

Bats have a very good sense of hearing.

6 NERVES

Our senses and nerves let the brain know what is going on, both outside and inside our bodies. The brain can then direct the body to find food when we are hungry, drink water when we are thirsty, sleep when we are tired, keep away from danger, and seek help if we are ill. The nervous system never stops working.

NERVE CELLS

The nervous system works in a similar way to a telephone network. The "wiring" is made up of cells – the microscopic building blocks that form all parts of the body. Nerve cells are called neurones. Like other cells, they have a nucleus and internal cellular parts (organelles). But they cannot reproduce themselves, which most other body cells can, and they have only limited powers of repair if damaged.

Arms extend from a neurone's cell body. Dendrites are thin branching arms that exchange signals with other neurones. Dendrons collect signals from sensory receptors (for example, heat receptors in the skin). Axons carry signals from the cell body to other neurones or to organs such as muscles. Nerve cells connect with each other at junctions called synapses.

The "skin" that covers each nerve cell is called the cell membrane. It is this that carries the tiny electrical signals which make up nerve messages. As a message travels along a cell, electrically charged atoms (ions) of sodium and potassium move through the membrane, causing a change in its electrical charge. Axons are wrapped in a sheath of special insulating material, so that their signals do not get mixed up with signals in neighbouring neurones – neurones are often bundled closely together. The insulating material, called myelin, is also made of special cells, called Schwann cells. All the way along the axon, where Schwann cells meet, there are narrow parts called the nodes of Ranvier. Here the signals are

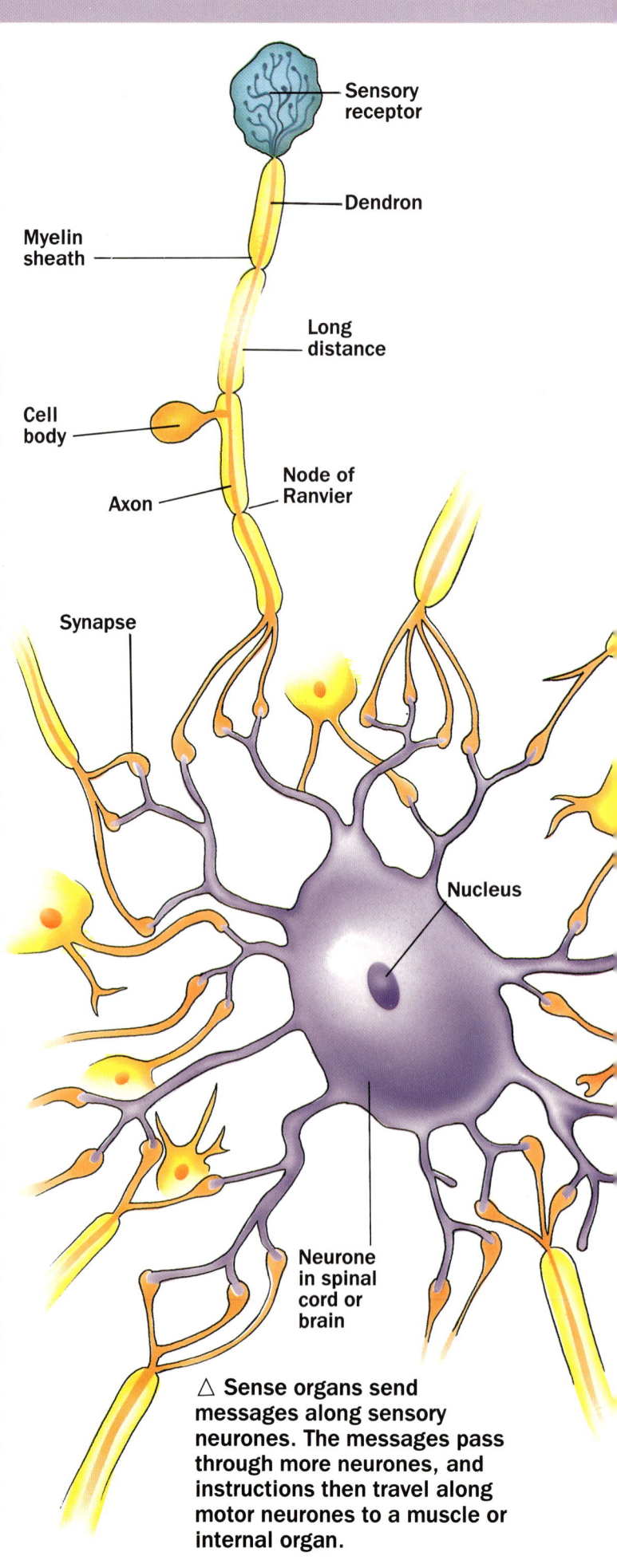

△ Sense organs send messages along sensory neurones. The messages pass through more neurones, and instructions then travel along motor neurones to a muscle or internal organ.

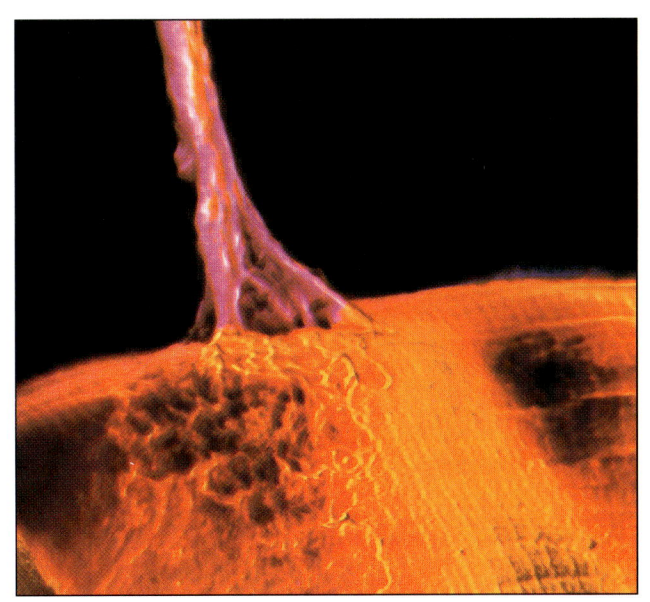

"boosted" as they jump from node to node.

Nerve cells communicate with each other at the synapses. When an electrical signal arrives at a synapse, it releases special chemicals. The chemicals travel across the microscopic gap between the cells to the next neurone. When the chemicals reach the next neurone, the cell is "fired". The signal then travels on, along its cell membrane. Once a neurone has fired, there is a pause before it recovers and can be fired again.

There are so many neurones and connections in the whole nervous system that it would soon become jammed with messages unless it had some sort of filtering system. Filtering takes place at the synapses. A neurone will transmit a signal only if it receives enough signals from other neurones to suggest it is an important message.

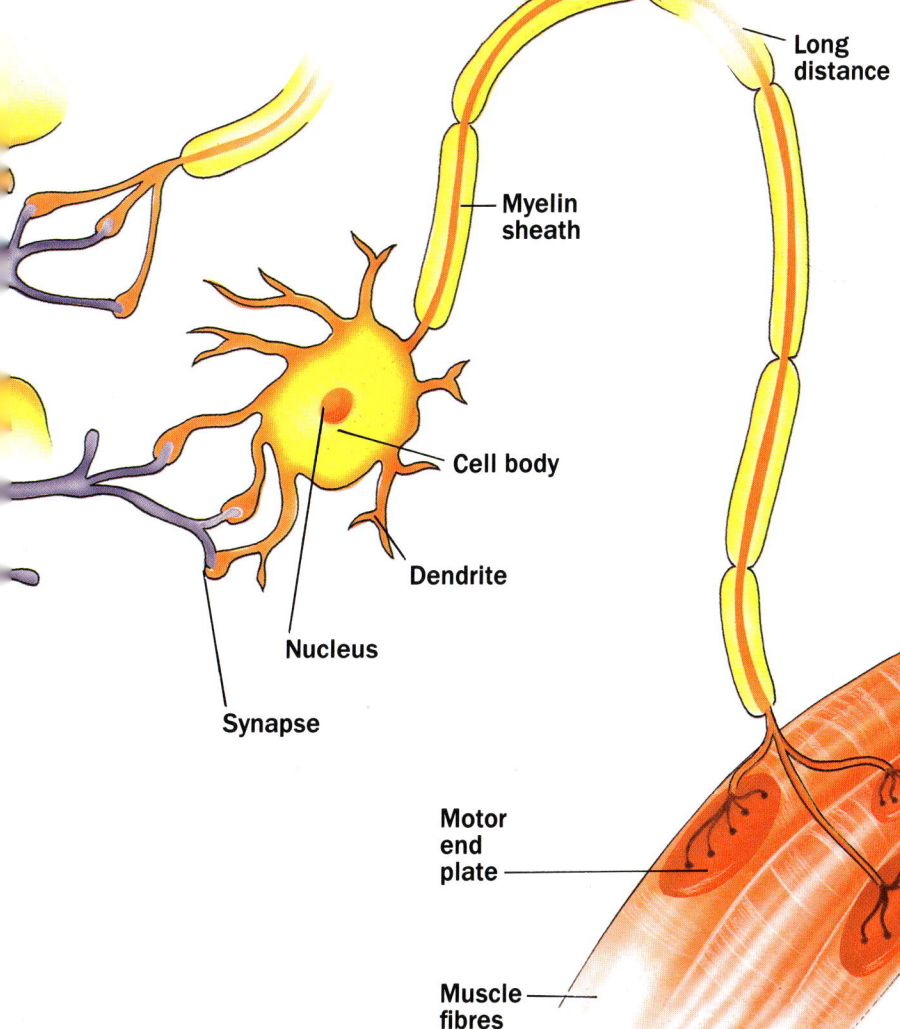

△ Where motor neurones reach a muscle, they branch into several strands. When a nerve message arrives, the strands release chemicals. These chemicals give a signal for the muscle to contract.

Long distance
Myelin sheath
Cell body
Dendrite
Nucleus
Synapse
Motor end plate
Muscle fibres

A NERVE CIRCUIT

Wire a drawing pin to a torch bulb. Connect the bulb to a battery, and wire the battery to another drawing pin. Make a switch from a metal paperclip. When the switch completes the circuit, the bulb lights up. This is rather like a sense organ passing a nerve signal to the brain.

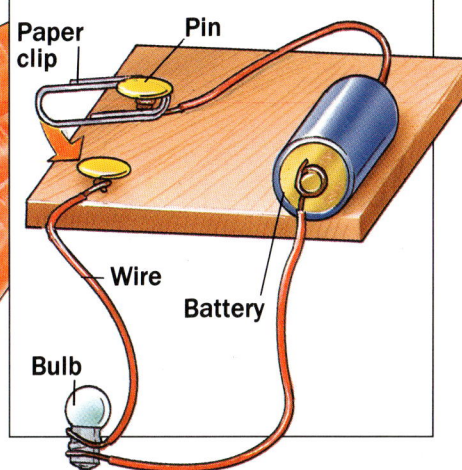

Paper clip
Pin
Wire
Battery
Bulb

8 THE NERVOUS SYSTEM

Sensory neurones carry messages from the sense organs to the brain. Motor neurones carry signals from the brain to the muscles. These two make up the peripheral nervous system. The brain and spinal cord form the central nervous system. The autonomic nervous system controls the internal organs.

PERIPHERAL AND CENTRAL

Peripheral nerves travel throughout the body. Sensory neurones carry messages from the skin, eyes, ears and other sense organs to the central nervous system. Motor neurones carry instructions from the central nervous system to the muscles and internal organs. The peripheral nerves are made up of bundles of nerve fibres and their protective sheaths. Usually, both motor and sensory fibres are mixed together in a single nerve.

The peripheral nerves join the spinal cord in pairs. They enter the spine between each of the bones. There are 31 pairs of peripheral nerves. They go to the skin, muscles and most other body organs. Each half of a pair goes to the organs in one half of the body. There are also 12 pairs of cranial nerves in the skull. These are also peripheral nerves. They carry information between the eyes, ears, mouth, nose and skin of the head and the brain.

The spinal cord is a thick bundle of nerves. It passes through a tube formed by the lined-up holes in the backbones, (or vertebrae). At the top end, it passes through a hole at the base of the skull and joins to the brain.

At the spinal cord, the peripheral nerves split so that most sensory neurones enter the cord from the back and the motor neurones enter from the front. Within the H-shaped centre of the cord (known as grey matter), the neurones are connected to thousands of other neurones. Some of these neurones travel up and down the cord.

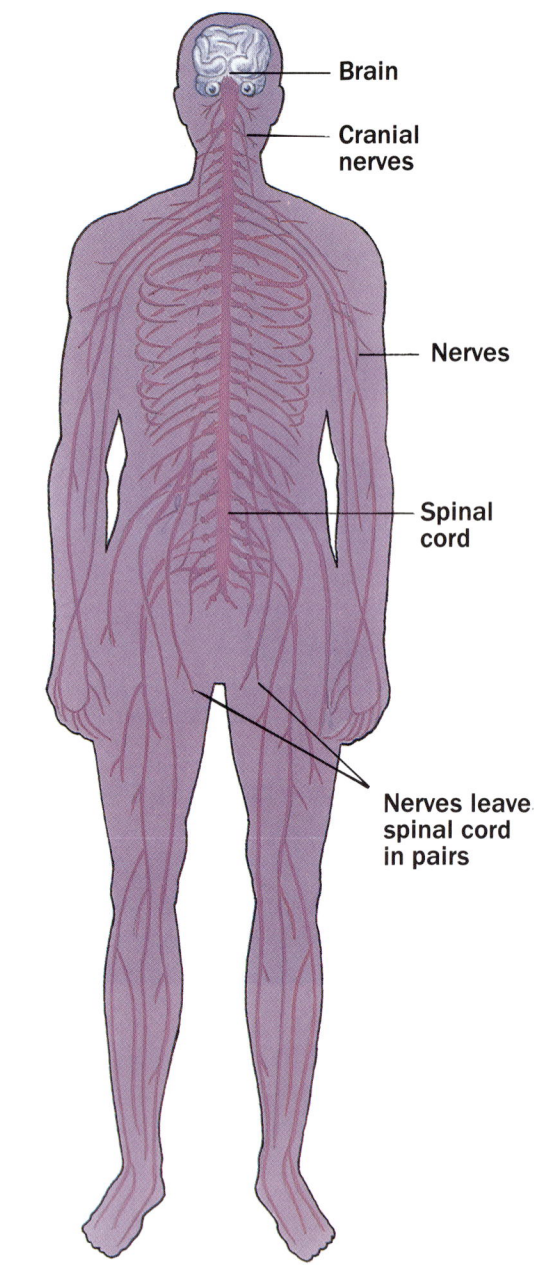

△ The main nerves of the body's nervous system.

DID YOU KNOW?

● Altogether the nerves in the body of an adult human being stretch for 75 kilometres.
● The average human brain weighs about 1,400 grams — but 80 per cent of that is water!
● A child's brain is 90 per cent of its adult size by the sixth birthday.

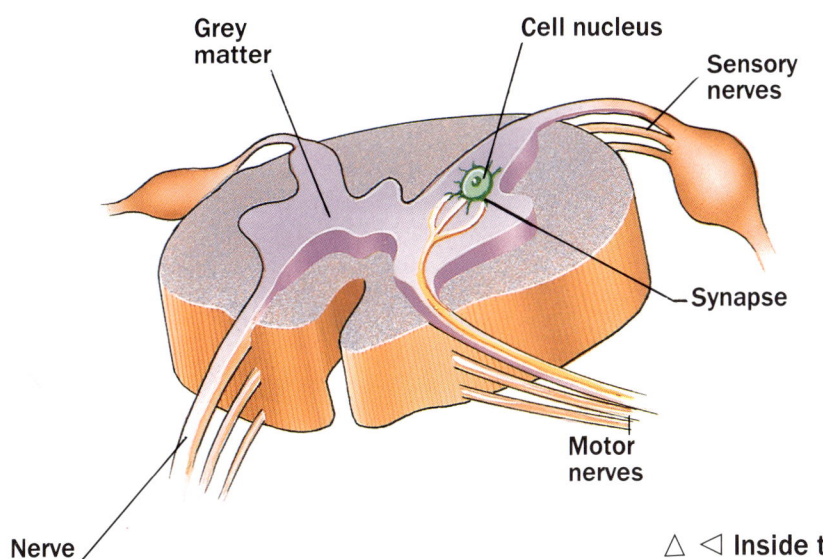

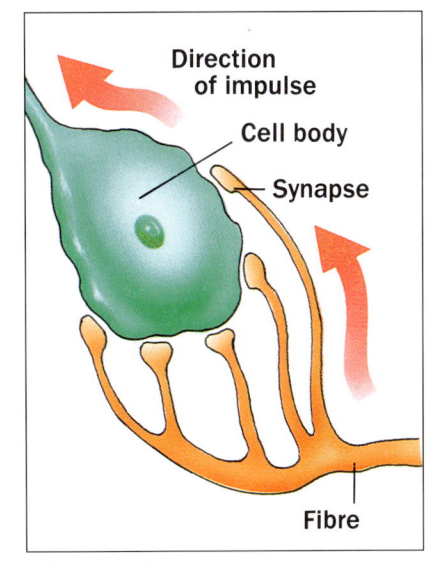

REFLEX CONTROL

The body has several kinds of automatic control system. Some involve chemicals (hormones) that pass round the body. Others involve the autonomic nervous system (see page 28). Quick changes that involve the peripheral nervous system are called reflex actions.

Reflex actions usually happen in response to a particular stimulus. An example is sneezing, which happens in response to an itch in the nose. Another example is if you put your hand on something very hot, you pull your hand away automatically, without even thinking about it. You have little or no control over most reflex actions, and it is difficult to stop them happening.

The spinal cord is responsible for many reflex actions. There is no time for the brain to be involved because the actions must happen so quickly. Messages from sensory nerves enter the cord. They are sent straight out again through motor nerves to the muscles. The brain is also involved in some reflex actions. These actions mostly concern those parts of the peripheral nervous system that are connected directly to the brain and not to the spinal column.

△ ◁ Inside the spinal cord, the white matter is where the nerve fibres pass up and down the cord. Peripheral nerve fibres pass into the grey matter, where they make connections with many other neurones. Nerve signals travel in one direction, from the terminals of the axon to the cell body, then on along the next axon.

TEST YOUR REFLEXES

Sit with your legs crossed and get a friend to tap your knee, just below the knee-cap. Your leg will kick. The tendon that attaches your knee-cap to your shin bone contains sensors that send a message to the spinal cord. This is part of our automatic walking mechanism. The message comes straight back and tells your foot to move forward quickly.

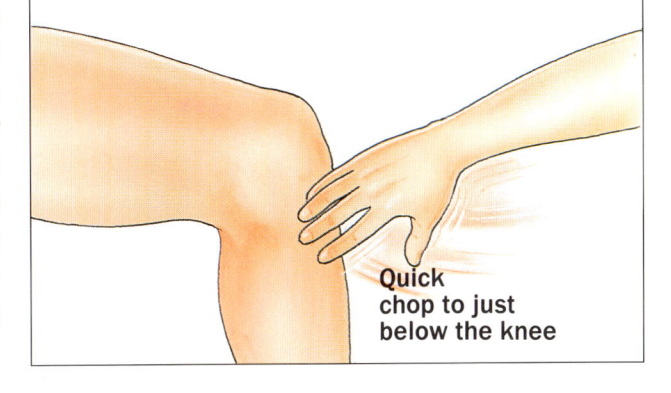

Quick chop to just below the knee

10 THE BRAIN

The brain is the central control "computer" of the nervous system. It is where information arriving from the sense organs (such as the eyes) is filtered and sorted, decisions are made, and the performance of the organs of the body is monitored and controlled. It is also where our thoughts occur.

STRUCTURE OF THE BRAIN

The brain occupies most of the inside of the skull. It is protected and cushioned by bones and by three layers of tissue called the meninges. The outer of these is the thickest and toughest, the dura mater. The next layer is called the arachnoid layer and is spongy, carrying blood vessels. Within this layer is the cerebrospinal fluid, a clear liquid that nourishes the central nervous system and helps to protect it. The innermost layer is the pia mater, a fine membrane that follows the shape of the brain.

The brain stem, at the base of the brain, is made up of two main parts: the medulla oblongata and the pons. Behind is the wrinkly cerebellum, which is joined to the cerebrum by the midbrain.

The cerebrum at the top is divided into two halves, the cerebral hemispheres. Its surface, the cerebral cortex, is made of grey matter (like that in the spine) and is thrown into walnut-like folds. The two halves of the cerebrum are joined by large bundles of nerve fibres that cross within the corpus callosum. To the sides of the corpus callosum there are spaces that contain the nourishing cerebrospinal fluid. In the centre of the brain is the thalamus most of the information from the senses to the cerebrum passes through this. Also at the centre is the hypothalamus, which is concerned with basic urges such as hunger and thirst. Near to the hypothalamus is the pituitary gland. This gland produces many hormones, and these control many different processes in the body.

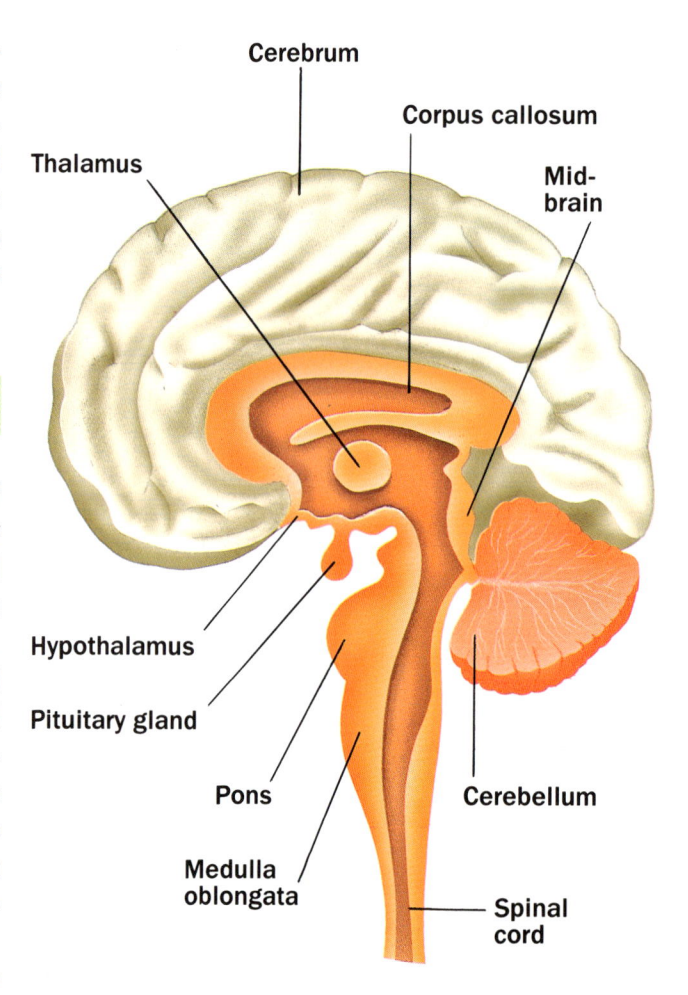

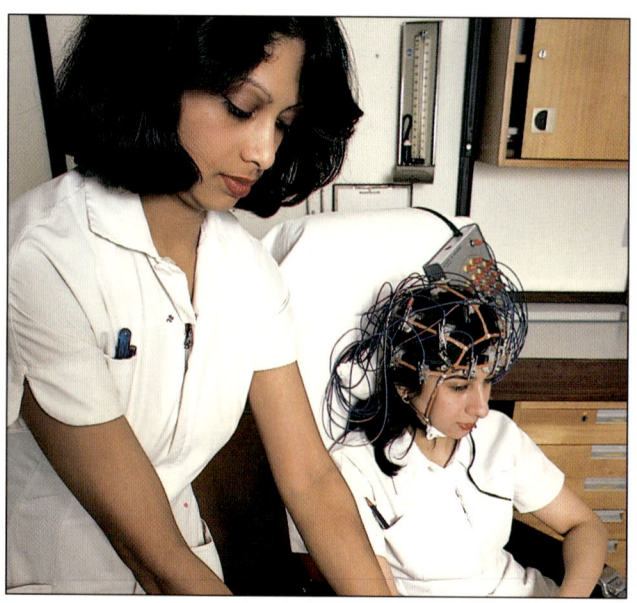

△ The electrical signals of the neurones in the cerebral cortex can be measured and recorded by an EEG (electroencephalography) machine. The wave patterns produced are different when the brain is at rest and when it is thinking.

◁ A human brain has the same parts as the brains of all animals with backbones. But a large cerebrum is found only in mammals. Other parts of the brain control the basic functions that keep an animal alive and well.

▽ The colours show what various parts of the cerebrums of these mammals are used for. They indicate which senses are important to the animal. For example, smell is important to rats, and humans have plenty of non-specific brain for thinking.

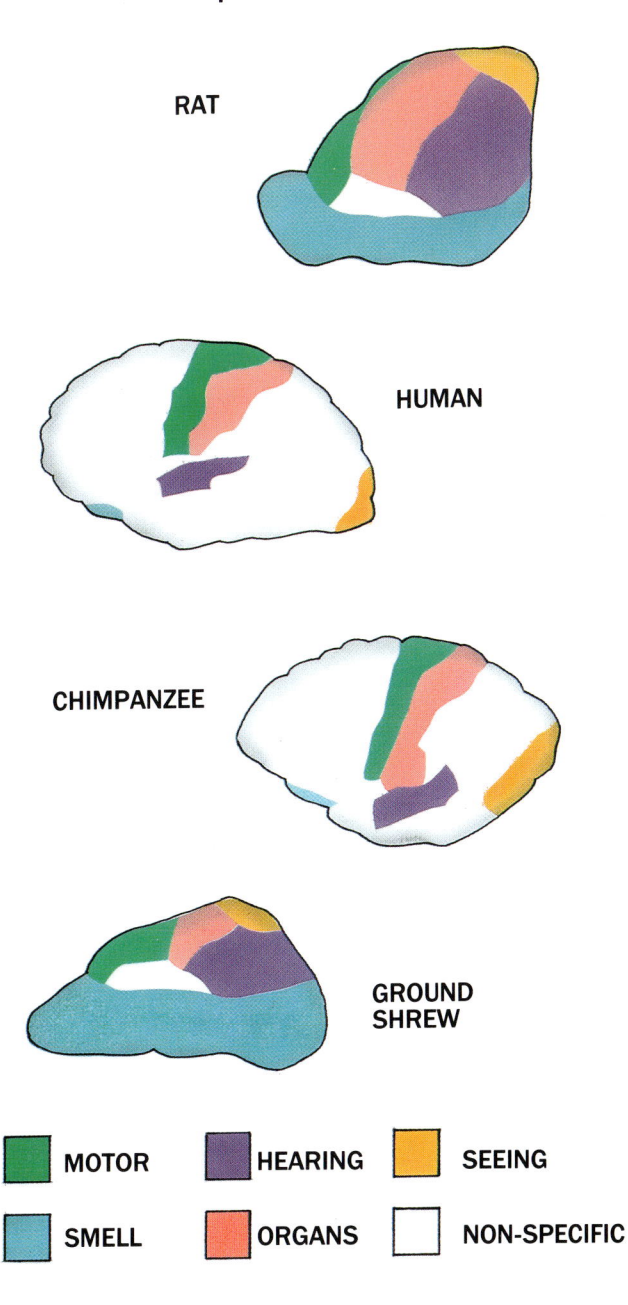

RAT

HUMAN

CHIMPANZEE

GROUND SHREW

- ■ MOTOR
- ■ SMELL
- ■ HEARING
- ■ ORGANS
- ■ SEEING
- □ NON-SPECIFIC

FUNCTIONS OF THE BRAIN

Each part of the brain has a different function. The brain stem — the medulla and pons — are the most "primitive" of the brain parts. They control the basic functions that keep the body alive. They monitor the working of the internal organs such as the heart, lungs and the intestines. Here also the nerve fibres from the body enter the brain from the spinal column.

The cerebellum is responsible for the unconscious control of balance and movements. It co-ordinates the many muscles that are used in complex patterns of movement, such as walking, running, jumping, playing the piano or riding a bicycle.

The midbrain co-ordinates movements of the eyes, head and body to follow the sources of sights and sounds.

The cerebral hemispheres are where information from the senses is analyzed, decisions are made, and instructions sent out for all of our conscious activities. Here we calculate, appreciate, make comparisons and memorize our experiences. Thoughts, plans and communications all start here. Each of these functions takes place in a particular area of the folds of the cerebral cortex.

THE CRUMPLED CORTEX

The cerebral cortex is made up of thousands of millions of nerve fibres. If they were arranged on a flat surface, they would cover almost four square metres. Stick two large sheets of newspaper together. Crumple them up to see how they could fit inside the skull.

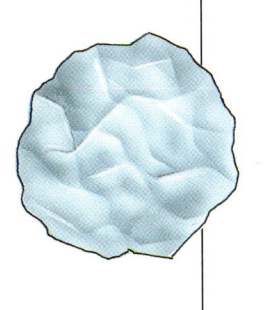

12 PERCEPTION

Perception — the way we recognize and understand things — takes place in the cortex of the brain. Scientists know that these processes must involve millions of neurones, all carrying electrical signals and connected together by synpases. But it is still not clear exactly how the mechanism of perception works.

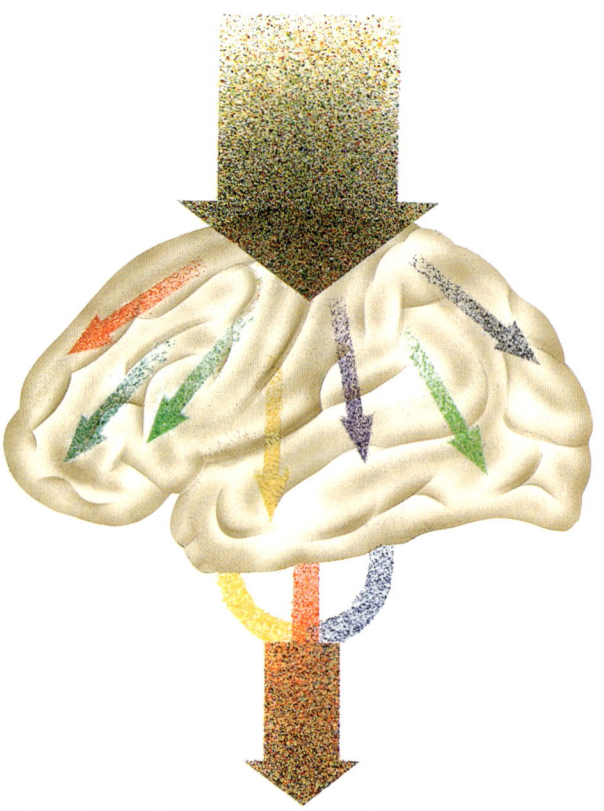

FILTERING INFORMATION

The vast amount of information from the senses that the brain receives is carefully filtered before it comes to our conscious perception. This allows more important signals to be filtered from less important ones. Each neurone has connections to and from many other neurones. Information is filtered at each connection because a neurone will not transmit a new signal unless it receives signals from several other neurones.

When the signals arrive in the correct part of the cerebral cortex, different neurones are fired by different types of information. For example, in the visual part of the cortex some neurones respond only to signals received when the eye sees a vertical line, some only respond to horizontal lines and some only to diagonal lines.

△ Information coming into the brain is filtered and directed to the correct part of the cortex. Here the information is interpreted and directions sent out to the body if any action is needed in response.

△ The brain monitors all sensory information, but we notice only important things such as hearing our name.

INTERPRETING INFORMATION

Interpretation of the meaning of incoming information is done by comparing the pathways that signals have taken and the responses to them on the cortex with memorized experiences. The brain often makes guesses based on previous experience. But because we very quickly learn about the world around us when we are babies, this way of doing things seems to work very well.

We are conscious of normal background sights, sounds and smells. But our attention is drawn particularly to unexpected changes, such as a new smell — is it something burning? When the information has been interpreted, the brain must decide what is to be done and what instructions to send out.

THOUGHTS AND EMOTIONS

The way that we think and feel makes up our individual personalities. We are social animals, that is, much of our time is spent dealing with other people. Our personalities are important to social communication. Conscious thought, which involves reasoning and planning, occurs in a large part of the cortex. It involves both halves (hemispheres) and uses information from all parts of the brain. Thinking involves language, information from the sense organs and memories. Emotions such as fear, anger, pleasure and sorrow also affect the way we think.

Deep within the brain is the limbic system. It is made up of part of the cortex and the hypothalamus. This is the emotional centre of the brain. Our emotions are altered by information coming from the sensory organs and also by changes within the body such as hunger or hormonal levels.

The cerebral hemispheres are in a way like two brains, and each can function on its own. But each half has its strengths and weaknesses. They work together to produce the mix of things that we are good at. The left hemisphere is the logical, reasoning side. It is good at calculating and is responsible for language. The right side is more artistic and creative. It is capable of appreciation and imagination. Everyone can do all these things, but the side of the brain that is stronger in us makes us better at some things than at others.

△ The right hemisphere is the more artistic side of the brain and is the stronger side in creative people.

OPTICAL ILLUSIONS

Optical illusions are fun, and they also show how the brain interprets images by comparing them with things it knows and then making guesses. The silhouette can be two faces or one vase. Which of the two flower centres is the largest? Measure them. The triangle is an impossible shape. But when you look at it your brain will try to see a three-dimensional figure.

14 MEMORY

Memory is important because it allows the brain to interpret information. It also allows us to think, speak and reason. The memory is based deep within the brain in regions known as the hippocampus and the amygdala. Scientists are only just beginning to have an understanding of how memory works.

LEARNING

Learning means memorizing information that can alter future behaviour. We learn things all the time. Babies start learning about their family and home as soon as they are born. Most children have learned half of everything they will ever know by the time they are six or seven years old. They can talk, walk and use a pencil. They understand thousands of words and are learning to read. After this stage, learning is mainly improving and expanding these abilities.

Learning something new is hard at first. It takes a lot of concentration to set up the nerve pathways involved in a new operation. Each time the pathways are used, they become stronger until the operation is almost automatic. This is how learning works. Practice really does make perfect.

There are also other types of learning. For instance when the school dinner bell goes your mouth waters — you are producing the saliva and other digestive juices that will be needed when your dinner arrives. This is called conditioning. It also happens when we get used to things around us such as bright lights, wearing clothes or hearing a clock ticking. After a while, you stop noticing these things. This type of learning helps to prevent the brain from being overloaded with unimportant information.

△ Learning to ride a bicycle is very difficult to start with. You have to co-ordinate your muscles with your sense of balance and it takes a lot of practice. But once you have managed to learn it, you will never forget.

◁ Walking is an inbuilt skill, but a baby's bones and muscles need to be strong enough before it can start. Practice is needed to improve the balance and co-ordination that is necessary.

LONG-TERM AND SHORT-TERM

Learning depends on the memory. We use our memories all the time to understand what goes on around us, because most things that happen have happened before. When someone is talking to you, you have to remember the beginning of each sentence so that you can understand it at the end. We can remember not only words but also music, images we have seen, smells, tastes and feelings. When we experience these things again, they often bring back memories which include lots of information about the time we first had the experience.

Memory depends on three stages. The first is the gathering of information, the second is storage and the third is retrieving the information. Information from the senses goes first into the short-term memory, where small amounts of information, such as a telephone number, are stored for about a minute. The short-term memory is very small. Any new information that has to be stored pushes out what is already in it.

If the information in the short-term memory is reinforced often enough by repetition, the information passes into the long-term memory. This memory stores everything we ever learn, consciously or unconsciously. It can hold as much information as the memory banks of a thousand of the biggest computers.

When we forget things, it is either because the memory part of the brain has been damaged or because the recall system is not working properly — perhaps because it has not been used for a while. Techniques to improve peoples' memories are based on improving the recall sytem. It is often easier to recall information if it is part of a meaningful sequence. So people use sentences such as *Richard Of York Gave Battle In Vain* to make it easy to remember the colours of the rainbow: *Red, Orange, Yellow, Green, Blue, Indigo, Violet*.

△ It is easier to learn things by doing them and gaining first-hand experience. For example, doing science experiments lets us see what happens for ourselves.

MEMORY TEST

Try this memory game and see how good your memory is. Put several ordinary household articles on a tray and look at them for two minutes. Then get a friend to remove one item while you are not looking. See if you can remember what is missing. To make it harder, put more things on the tray or get your friend to remove more than one item at a time.

16 NERVES TO MUSCLES

The brain sends out motor messages which travel down the spinal cord and along the nerve bundles to all parts of the body. The muscles contract in certain orders and at different levels of power. They are monitored and co-ordinated by the brain and can carry out the most delicate or the heaviest of jobs.

MOVEMENT

Muscles move the rigid bones that make up the skeleton. Muscles have tendons at each end, which are attached to bones on either side of a joint. When a muscle contracts it becomes shorter and fatter, and pulls the bones towards each other, causing the joint to bend.

Muscles are made of tiny cells shaped like long thin fibres. Several fibres are bundled together and wrapped in a membrane. Several bundles are in turn wrapped in a further membrane to form the muscle. The wrapping membranes continue at each end of the muscle to become the tendons.

Muscle fibres contain long, thin molecules of chemicals called actin and myosin. These molecules are arranged as stacks of actin and stacks of myosin. The stacks are linked together because the ends of the actin molecules lie between the ends of the myosin molecules. When a muscle contracts, the two types of molecule crawl along each other using special chemical bonds as "legs". In this way, the stacks of molecules are pulled closer together and the muscle fibre gets shorter. When lots of fibres within a muscle get shorter, the whole muscle contracts.

Each muscle fibre has several plates on its surface that are the ends of motor neurones. These plates are similar to the synapses between neurones, and they release special chemicals (called transmitters). These chemicals start an electrical signal in the muscle fibre which causes it to contract. A muscle often contains both contracting and resting fibres at the same time. The power of the muscle is increased when more fibres are caused to contract.

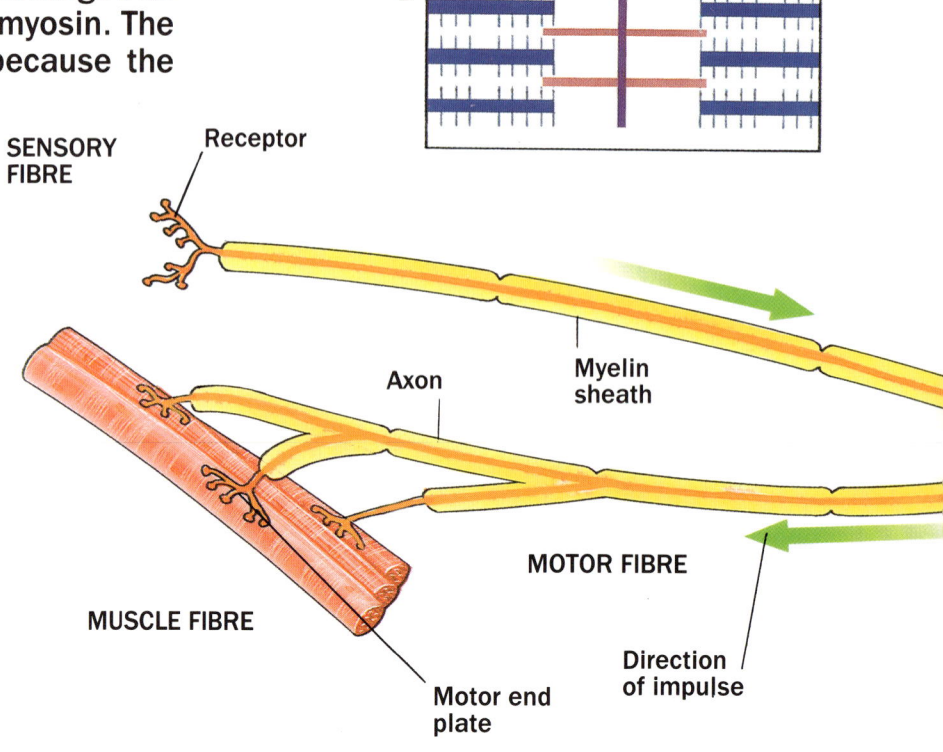

▷ Seen under a microscope, stacks of actin and myosin molecules in a muscle fibre appear as bands. Chemical bonds, acting like "legs", move them together when a muscle contracts (A) and then apart (B).

The contraction is stimulated by the end plates of motor nerves. The signals often come from the brain, travelling through the spinal cord. But in complex actions, such as walking, the signals may be part of reflex actions (see page 9). In this case, signals from sensory nerves travel through the spinal cord and straight out again to a muscle.

CONTROL

Contracting muscles must be finely controlled to perform tasks such as riding a bicycle, writing a word or playing a musical instrument. This control is produced by a system of nerves between the muscles, the sense organs and the brain. For example, walking involves the muscles of the legs, lower back and arms. The brain sends out messages to instruct all these muscles to begin working. But the walking process is controlled by many parts of the body.

Walking is monitored by the organs of balance in the ear to make sure that we are not falling over; by the stretch receptors within the muscles so that we know how hard they are pulling; by the pressure sensors in the skin of the soles of the feet; and by the eyes to see if we are going to crash into anything.

All this sensory information goes to the brain. The brain then modifies the instructions it is sending out to the muscles so that they act in the necessary way. This happens continuously thousands of times every second with hardly any conscious thought. We can even do other things while we are walking, such as unwrapping a sweet, talking or even playing an instrument.

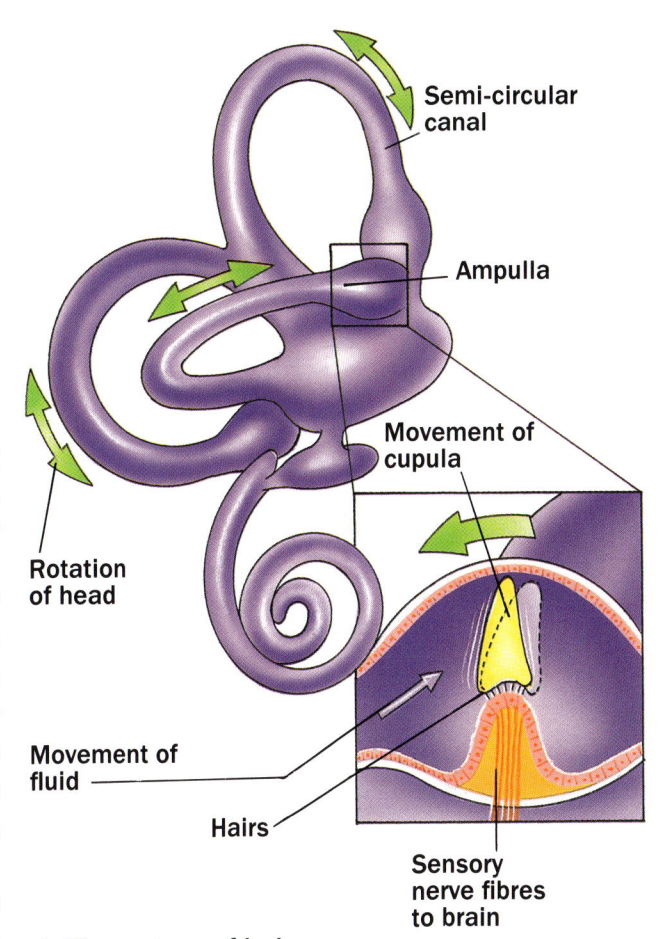

△ The organs of balance are the three semi-circular canals in each ear. They contain fluid. Each of the canals has a cupula at one end. When the head moves, the fluid moves, and this in turn moves the cupula. When the cupula moves, it bends tiny hairs that connect to nerve endings.

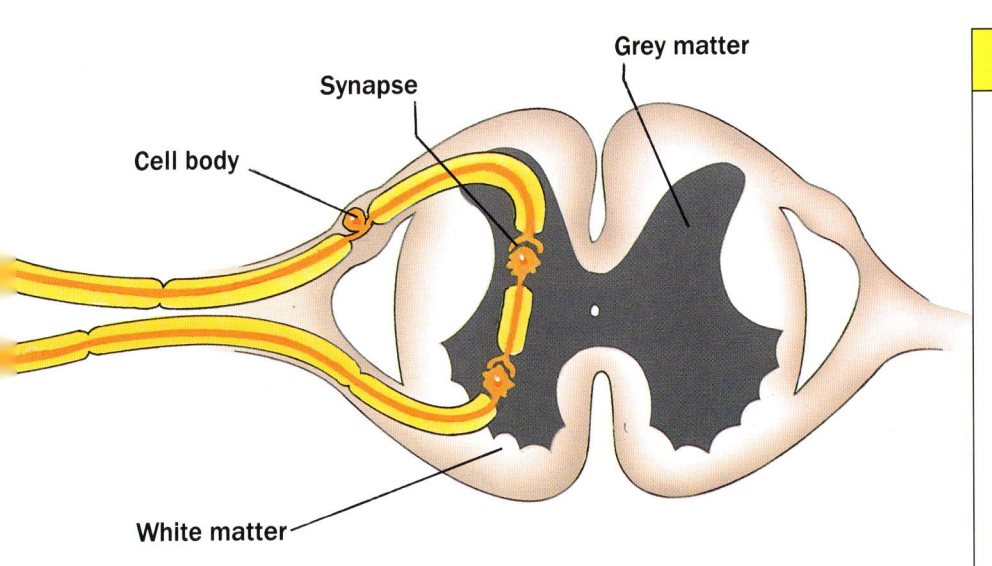

SPINAL CORD

DIZZINESS

Try spinning round and round on one spot in an open space. When we spin, the messages that the brain gets from the eyes do not match up with the messages from the organs of balance in the ears. We feel dizzy, we cannot stand upright properly and we may feel slightly sick.

18 SEEING

The brain keeps in touch with what is going on around us by means of the sense organs. The main senses are sight, hearing, touch, taste and smell. Perhaps our best sense is that of sight. We can see in daylight and to some extent at night; we see in colour and in three dimensions (width, depth and height).

THE EYE

The eyeball is made up of three layers. The sclera is the outer layer to which the muscles that move the eyeball are attached. At the front of the eye, the sclera becomes the transparent cornea. The cornea is covered by the conjunctiva, a membrane that lubricates and cleans the surface of the eye.

The middle layer is the choroid layer, which contains blood vessels and a pigment to prevent reflection of light. At the front of the eye, behind the cornea, the choroid layer becomes the ciliary muscles, which support and focus the lens of the eye. The muscular iris, which covers most of the lens, also comes from the choroid layer. The hole in the middle of the iris is the pupil.

The third layer, the retina, covers the rear part of the inside of the eye. It contains light-sensitive cells — the rods and cones — and the nerve fibres leading from them. The fibres travel to the brain along the optic nerve.

The front of the eye is filled with clear liquid called the aqueous humour, while the main part is filled with a clear jelly called the vitreous humour.

The eye operates on a similar principle to a camera. Light, reflected from the things around us, enters the eye through the pupil. It falls on the retina, forming an upside-down image, focused by the cornea and the lens. The rods and cones are sensory cells which are stimulated by light. The rods are sensitive to light intensity, light and dark. The cones in the fovea respond to colour.

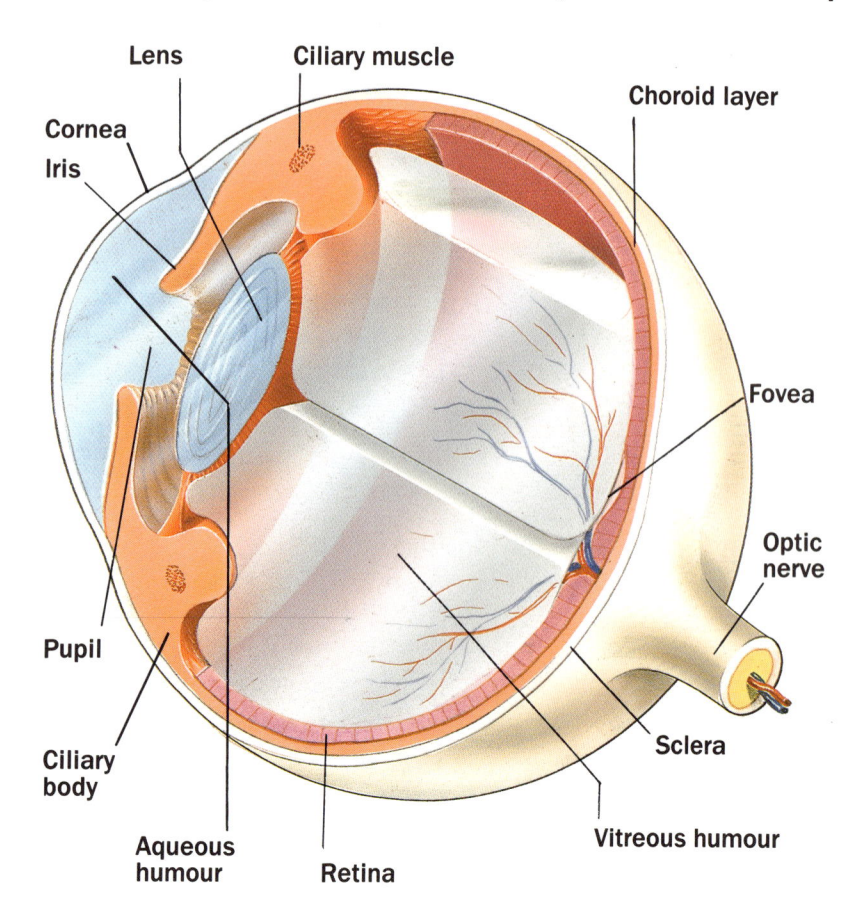

◁ The lens of the eye bulges when the ciliary body contracts. Light from near objects is focused on the retina by a bulging lens, and from distant objects by a thin lens.

DID YOU KNOW?

There is a blind spot at the back of the eye. This is where the nerve fibres leave for the optic nerve and there is no room for rods and cones. You can find your blind spot by closing your left eye and concentrating on the cross. Move the book nearer to you until the dot disappears. We do not usually notice the blind spot because we have two eyes.

COLOUR VISION

Human beings have very good colour vision, unlike many other animals. We see the sights around us in shades and mixtures of all the colours of the rainbow. Light travels in waves of different lengths and each wavelength is seen as light of a different colour. Things appear to be particular colours because of the type of light they reflect or give out.

The cones of the retina are responsible for our ability to see colour. There are three types. One type responds to red light, one to blue light and one to yellow light. Everything we see is made up of mixtures of these three colours. The brain analyses the signals coming from all three types of cone and interprets the colour in a similar way to mixing paint. For example, if a lot of yellow- and blue-sensitive cones are firing, but not many red-sensitive cones, in a particular part of the retina, then that part of the image is seen as green.

△ The rods and cones of the retina are arranged so that light must travel through their nerve connections before it reaches them. This seems a strange arrangement. But because the nerves are quite transparent and the brain can fill in any gaps in the image by guesswork, it works well.

PROJECT

Find out how the eye produces an image by making a box camera. You will need a shoe box with a lid. Cut a square out of one end and cover it with tracing paper. Make a tiny pin hole at the other end. Point the box at a strongly lit image. The image on the tracing paper will be upside down. This is the same in the eye.

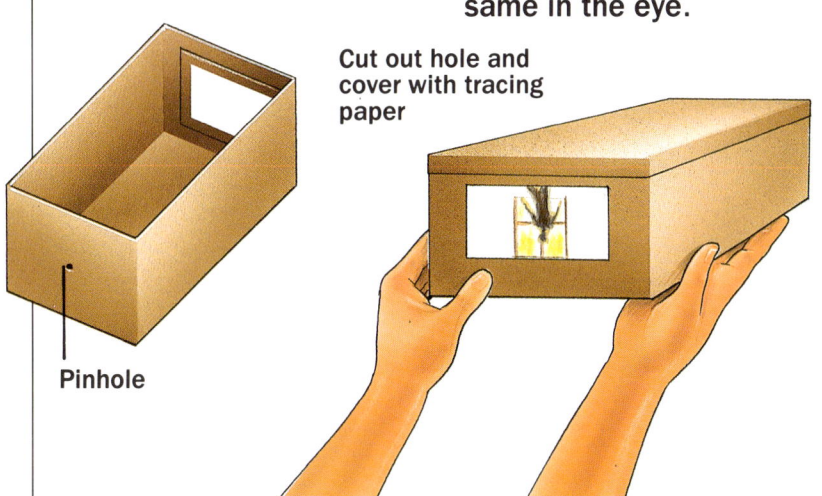

Pinhole

Cut out hole and cover with tracing paper

View a strong image against a well lit window

HEARING

Our sense of hearing, although not as good as that of many animals, serves us very well. Our hearing spans a great range of loudness, from the gentle patter of rain to a great clap of thunder. We can also hear a wide range of high and low notes. Most importantly, hearing enables us to speak to each other.

THE EAR

The ear flaps act as funnels that direct sound waves into the ear canals. The canals pass into the bone of the skull.

At the end of each canal is an ear drum, which vibrates when sound waves hit it. The vibrations pass along the three tiny bones which are connected to the inside of the eardrum. The last of these bones rests on another membrane which forms an oval window into the inner ear.

The inner ear consists of the semi-circular canals (which are concerned with balance) and a coiled cone called the cochlea. It is in the cochlea that the sounds are converted to electrical impulses the brain can understand.

△ Many animals have much better hearing than humans. Bat-eared foxes have huge ears that they can swivel in different directions to pick up the sounds of the insects and small animals they hunt. The large ears can "scoop up" a large amount of sound.

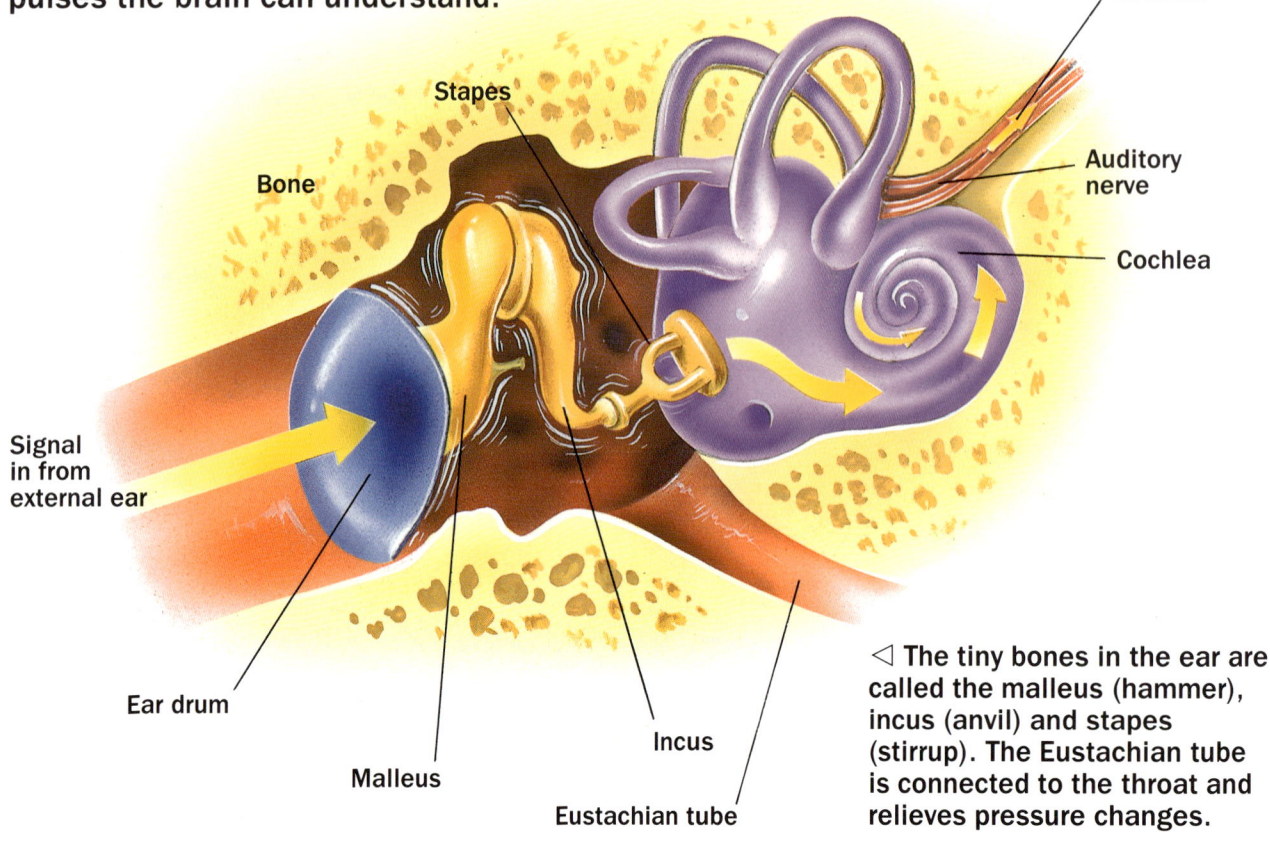

◁ The tiny bones in the ear are called the malleus (hammer), incus (anvil) and stapes (stirrup). The Eustachian tube is connected to the throat and relieves pressure changes.

Upper tube
Middle tube
Hair cells
Lower tube

Cross section through cochlea

Cochlear nerve – signal to brain

Organ of Corti

Signal to brain

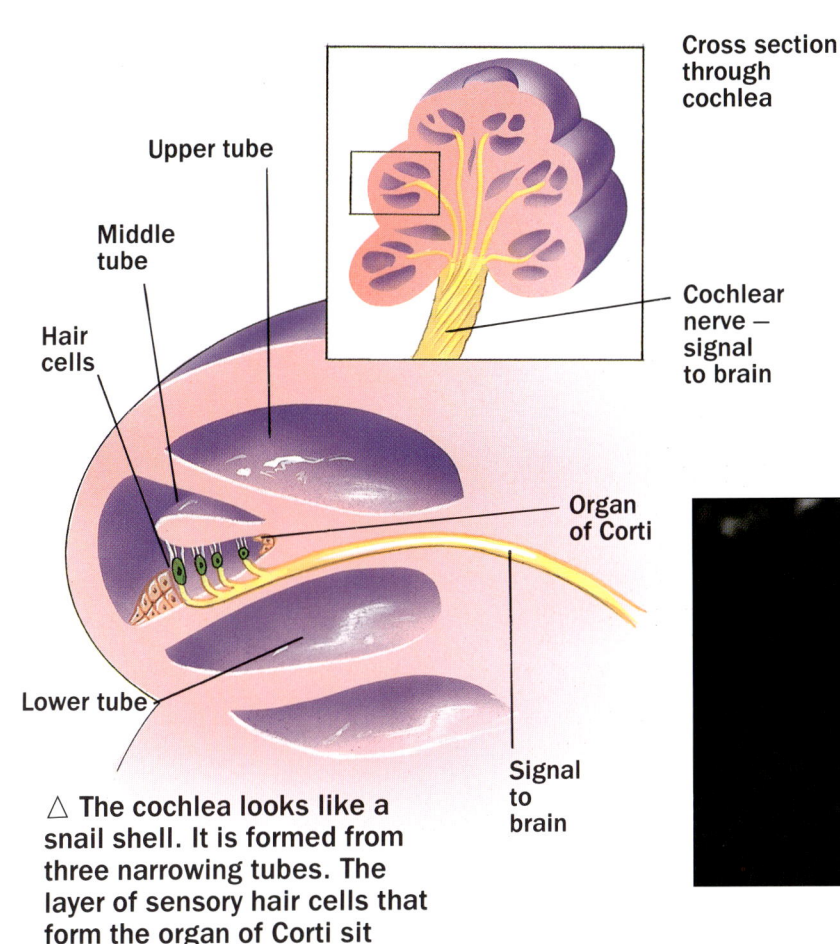

△ The cochlea looks like a snail shell. It is formed from three narrowing tubes. The layer of sensory hair cells that form the organ of Corti sit between two membranes.

PROJECT

Close your eyes and get a friend to move a ticking clock around the room. Can you tell where it is? Our brain works this out by comparing the signals from our two ears.

△ Like ears, microphones turn sounds into electrical signals.

THE SIGNALS

The cochlea is coiled round like a snail's shell. The inside of the cochlea is made up of three parallel tubes. The upper tube runs from the oval window to the point of the cone. The lower tube runs from the point of the cone back to a tiny round window at the wide end. These two tubes are connected at the end point of the cochlea and they contain watery perilymph fluid. The middle tube contains a fluid called endolymph, and is lined on the lower side by the sensory hair cells that form the organ of Corti.

The perilymph fluid carries sound vibrations from the oval window, along the cochlea and back to the round window. As the waves arrive at the round window, it bulges to relieve the pressure. The vibrations then pass on to the endolymph within the middle tube, the cochlea duct. The sensory hair cells respond to the vibrations in the endolymph and produce nerve signals. These travel along the auditory nerve to the brain, where they are interpreted as sounds.

The pitch of a sound is how high or low it sounds. It depends on the frequency of the sound waves (the number of vibrations per second). The ear can tell different pitches apart because different parts of the cochlea duct vibrate more strongly than others at different pitches. The narrow end of the cochlea duct vibrates more with low pitches, and the wide end of the duct vibrates more with high pitches.

The loudness of a sound depends on the amplitude (height) of the sound wave. Loud noises can damage the delicate membranes and sensitive cells in the ear. Amplitude is monitored as the vibrations pass through the tiny bones in the ear. Tiny muscles tighten to reduce the size and strength of the vibrations if the sound passing through is too loud.

SMELL

Our eyes and ears respond to the physical energy of light and sound. Smell and taste are concerned with the chemical nature of the world around us. The sense organ of smell is within the nose. It detects the chemicals in the air we breathe when they dissolve in the mucus that lines the nasal cavities.

THE SENSE OF SMELL

The olfactory (smell) organs are in the roof of the nasal cavity. They consist of the two olfactory bulbs. The area of each bulb involved is quite small — about one-and-a-half centimetres across. The bulbs lie just behind the bridge of the nose. The nasal cavity is lined with skin-covered ridges of bone called the turbinate bones. These direct the air we breathe over the olfactory bulbs and down to the back of the throat.

Beneath the olfactory bulbs are cells with tiny hairs. These hairs hang down into the mucus that covers the nasal cavity lining. When the hairs detect molecules of odour in the air, they trigger electrical impulses. The impulses pass to nerve cells in the olfactory bulb and then on to the brain.

Scientists are not exactly sure how we can recognize so many different smells. It is thought that there are at least seven different types of smell receptor cell, and possibly a lot more. The system may work like a "lock-and-key" mechanism. Each odour molecule has a certain shape, so that it only fits into a site on the sensory hairs of the type of cell that detects that particular smell.

The seven or more types of smell occur in different proportions in different smelly substances. The brain can tell by the mixture of signals it receives what the substance is. Everyone can smell as many as 3,000 different smells, but only experts, such as wine tasters and people who make perfume, have trained their brains to remember this many.

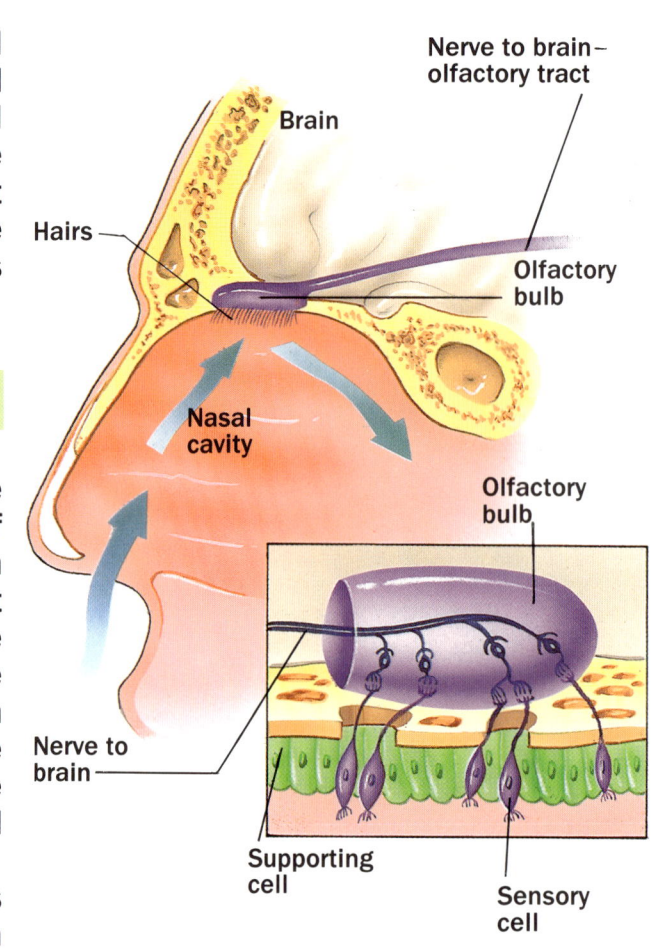

△ Smells are detected in the nasal cavities by the olfactory bulbs, which are extensions of the brain that carry the olfactory nerves.

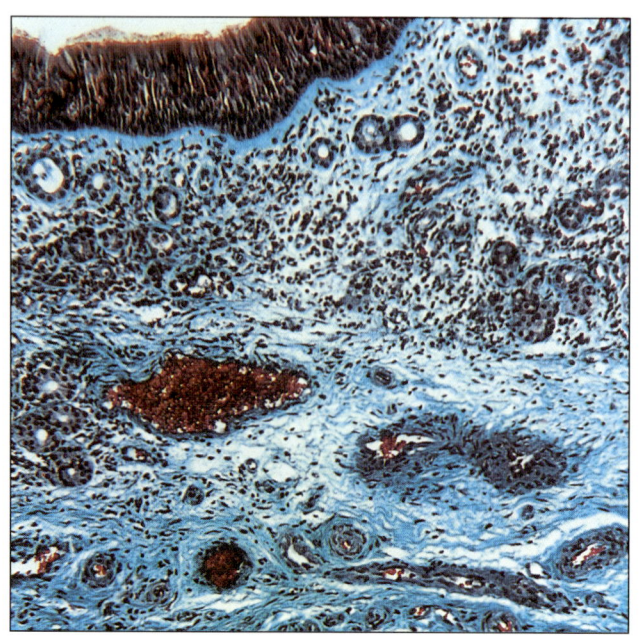

△ Fibres from the olfactory bulb can be seen (top left).

SMELLS

Today we use our sense of smell for pleasure rather than survival. We grow flowers with strong scents and we cook using lots of herbs and spices with mouth-watering smells. We spend a lot of time trying to hide our own body smells and replace them with perfumes. We even wash our clothes and linen in fragrant washing powders.

Animals such as dogs still use body smells as a way of recognizing a friend or an enemy. They also leave their smells all around their home territory. Body smells are very important to some animals when they want to reproduce. The smells they produce change when they are ready to mate. These sorts of smells are called pheromones and they carry very powerful messages.

Humans also produce pheromones, but they are much less important than in many animals. Experiments have shown that we are unconsciously aware of them. For example, one experiment showed that people tend to choose a seat in a waiting room if it has had a human pheromone sprayed onto it.

△ Humans do not have a good enough sense of smell to use when hunting. So they have trained dogs to point in the direction that the smell of an animal is coming from.

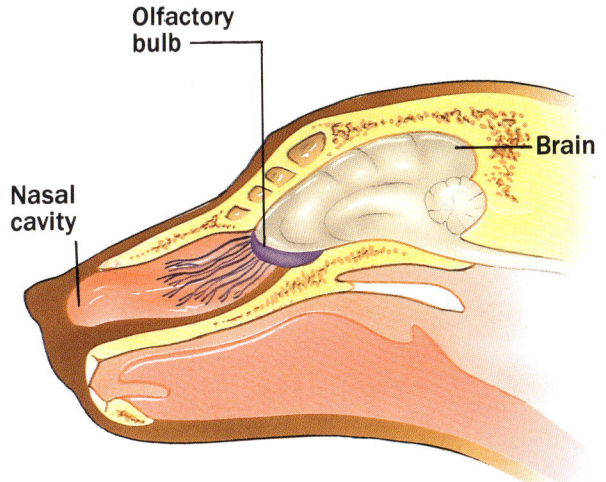

△ A dog's smell apparatus is much larger than ours and employs a much greater part of its brain. A dog's world is as full of smells as ours is full of sights. They recognize other dogs and people by their scents alone. They recognize smells on clothing and footprints, even though the person is long gone. They can also seek out chemical smells such as drugs and explosives.

△ Male lions wrinkle their noses when they smell a female pheromone.

24 TASTE

Our sense of taste is 10,000 times less sensitive than our sense of smell. The two senses work very closely together. Food never tastes quite the same when your nose is blocked up with the mucus of a cold. The tongue is the organ of taste. It can only detect four kinds of taste: sweet, sour, salt and bitter.

THE TONGUE

The tongue is a very muscular organ which serves to mix the food in the mouth. It pushes food between the grinding teeth and stirs in the saliva that begins the digestive process. The surface of the tongue is covered with tiny bumps (papillae). In pits between the papillae are groups of special cells. These groups are known as taste buds. The cells detect certain types of chemical when they enter a taste bud. They then send signals along nerve fibres to the brain. Taste buds can only detect chemicals when they are dissolved. One purpose of saliva is to make sure that the chemicals in food that make it taste do dissolve.

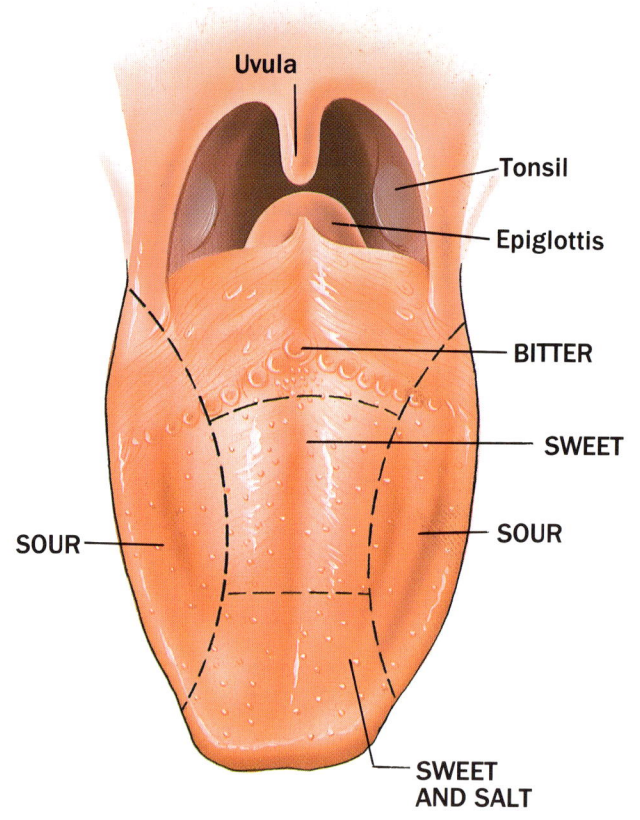

△ Different areas of the tongue have taste buds that respond to different tastes. The tongue is a muscle and can move in all sorts of ways so that food is mixed with saliva and every bit of the mixture touches every taste area.

TASTE AND SMELL

Test your senses of taste and smell and see how they work together. Cover your eyes and taste small amounts of salt and sugar with a peg on your nose. Can you tell the difference? Now try without the peg. Repeat the test with lemon juice and vinegar. Can you taste these tastes all over your tongue? Try placing them on the areas shown in the diagram of the tongue (at the top of the page) with your finger.

Try using a peg on your nose. Does it affect your taste?

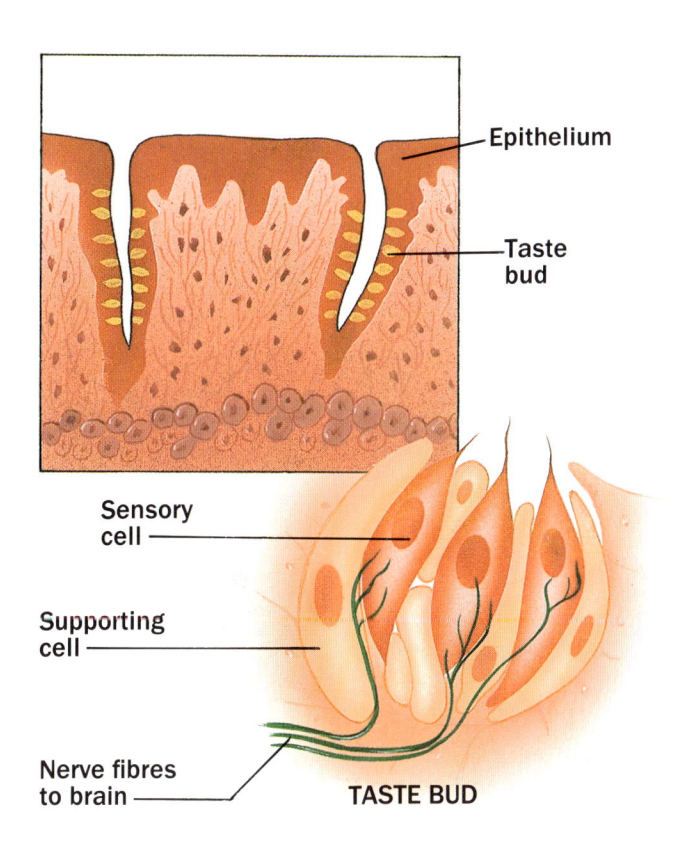

△ Taste buds nestle in pits on the tongue's surface. They are made up of chemical receptor cells which test the solution of food and saliva in the pit. There can be as many as 10,000 taste buds on the surface of the tongue.

△ The tongue is used to move and taste food.

TASTE AND DIGESTION

Mixtures of signals from taste buds in the tongue are sent to the brain. Here they are combined with information from the smell receptors in the nose. The brain analyzes the information and compares it to memorized tastes and smells. We can tell if the food is good or bad, and if we have eaten it before and enjoyed it. We may even suddenly be able to remember all sorts of things about the time and place in which we last experienced a particular taste.

Smell and taste not only serve to monitor our food, but they also get the digestive system going. Mouth-watering smells and tastes cause the salivary glands to produce saliva as soon as food is in our mouths. Chewing creates more taste and causes yet more saliva to be produced. Saliva helps to liquefy and lubricate the food for its journey down the digestive tract. It also contains enzymes — chemicals that begin to break down molecules in the food — and antiseptic substances to kill germs.

Tastes and smells quickly become less noticeable. A meal that tastes delicious for the first few mouthfuls may become quite ordinary by the time the plate is empty. The tastes have not changed, but we have become used to them.

DID YOU KNOW?

Taste buds are not only found on the tongue. They are also found on the soft palate at the back of the roof of the mouth, on the epiglottis and in the membranes lining the throat. There are many more taste buds in the mouth of a child than in an adult, and they continue to disappear as we get older.

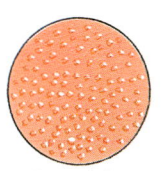

Age 14

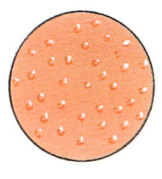

Age 60

TOUCH

We need to have information about things that are in contact with our bodies so that we can walk, hold things, avoid pain and injury, and touch other people. The skin that covers the surface of the body is full of nerve endings which respond to different amounts of pressure, pain and heat.

PRESSURE AND PAIN

The body is covered with about two square metres of skin. The skin's functions are to keep germs out and water and other body contents in, to help regulate temperature and to serve as a sense organ.

The skin consists of three layers. The lowest layer is fat. Above it is the dermis, in which blood vessels, nerves and nerve endings, sweat glands, the roots of hairs and oil-producing glands are found. The outer layer is the epidermis. It is constantly renewing itself as its outer dead layers are worn away.

The nerve endings found in the skin are of different types which respond to different stimuli. Those that are sensitive to pain caused by an injury have free ends with no capsule. The ends of light touch receptors are in capsules just under the epidermis. They are mostly in areas of skin which have little or no hair. The capsules of heavy pressure receptors are bigger and deeper in the skin and look like onions. There are many of them on the soles of the feet and palms of the hands. The hairs that cover the skin and scalp also have sensory nerves which respond when the hair is moved by an external force.

All these sensory nerve endings soon become used to the stimulus that initially makes them fire. We can feel our clothes when we put them on in the morning, but soon do not notice them unless they are very uncomfortable. We know when our feet first touch the floor but we forget them if we stand still for some time.

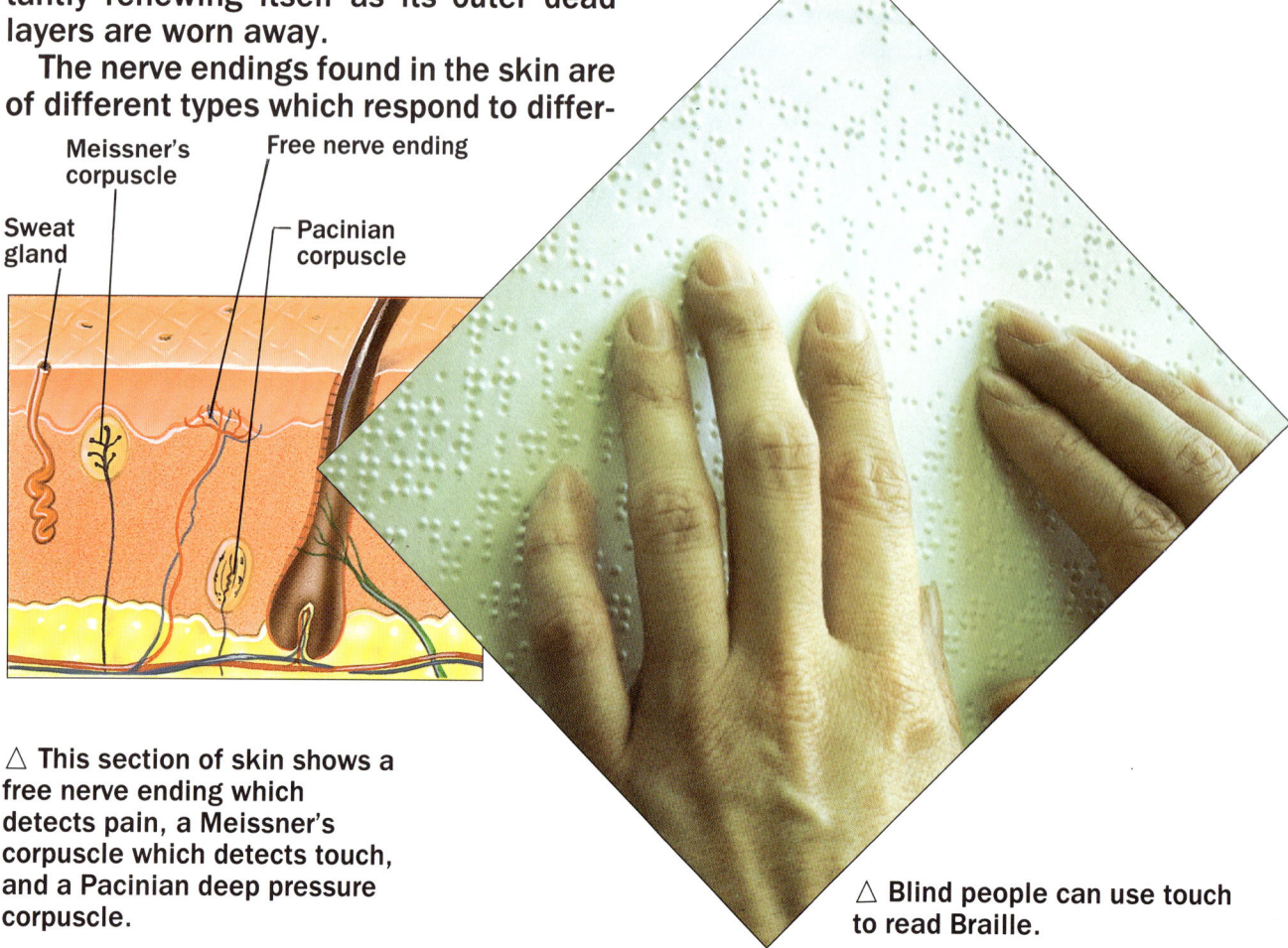

△ This section of skin shows a free nerve ending which detects pain, a Meissner's corpuscle which detects touch, and a Pacinian deep pressure corpuscle.

△ Blind people can use touch to read Braille.

HOT AND COLD

The nerve endings that feel cold are just below the epidermis. They are enclosed by large irregular capsules. The heat receptors are deep in the dermis and are shaped like a squashed sphere. The skin's sensitivity to temperature is very important because it is the main organ that controls body temperature.

When we get too cold, the skin increases its insulation qualities by raising all the little hairs on its surface. The hairs trap a layer of air which reduces heat loss. The blood vessels in the skin also become narrow to decrease the amount of warm blood at the surface; this also reduces heat loss.

If these measures do not produce an increase in the skin temperature and the body is likely to become too cold, instructions go the the muscles to shiver or contract and relax very rapidly. Shivering is an involuntary reflex outside our control. We cannot stop it even if we want to. It burns up energy, producing heat within the body just as running or stamping do. Our behaviour is also influenced by the lowering of skin temperature. We seek warmth by putting on more clothes or turning up the room heating.

△ Touch is one way for people to communicate.

When we get too hot, the hairs on the skin lie flat, increasing the circulation of air around the body. The blood vessels expand to allow more warm blood to flow near the skin's surface. Also, the sweat glands produce quantities of liquid. Sweat is a salty solution which also contains some waste products. We produce it most of the time in greater or lesser quantities. But when we are hot we can lose several litres of water a day through the skin. As the sweat evaporates, it draws heat from the skin and so causes it to cool down. This cools the blood near the surface.

DID YOU KNOW?

Our fingernails are not just useful for scratching. They also help to push the whole of the fingertip against the object we wish to feel. This increases the sensitivity of the fingertips.

△ A young orang-utan uses its lips to learn by touch.

INTERNAL SENSES

We are not conscious of the workings of our internal organs, but they have to be controlled to make sure they are working in the best way to keep us alive. The internal organs such as the gut, the kidneys and bladder, the liver, and the heart and lungs all have sensory nerve endings which monitor their functions.

INTERNAL MONITORING

The internal sensory nerve endings of the digestive system tell us when we need to empty the bowels or have something to eat. There are also nerve endings in the gut that respond to the pain of indigestion or infection.

The circulatory system is very complex. The blood carries nutrients and oxygen to the tissues to be used for energy; carbon dioxide to the lungs and waste to the kidneys for removal; and hormones which help to control the organs. The concentrations of substances in the blood must be monitored and kept at the right level. The heart and lungs must work harder to increase low levels of oxygen and remove high levels of carbon dioxide. The kidneys and bladder remove excess water from the blood, but if there is not enough water we feel thirsty.

△ Autonomic nerves prepare animals for action.

△ The autonomic nervous system makes us feel thirsty.

AUTONOMIC NERVOUS SYSTEM

The internal sensory system is involved with the process of keeping things in a steady state so that all the body organs work efficiently. This process is controlled by the autonomic nervous system. The nerves for this system run alongside the spinal cord within the backbone. They run to the heart and lungs, the gut and liver, the kidneys and bladder. They monitor these organs and give them instructions to increase or reduce activity, according to the body's needs. The whole process works automatically by reflex actions. But occasionally it must intrude on our thoughts when, for example, we need to eat or drink. There are two parts of the autonomic nervous system and they work against each other.

The two parts of the autonomic nervous system work in a "push-pull" way, each having an opposing effect. When the two parts are acting equally, there is no effect. But when one part acts more strongly than the other, the activities of organs change. One part of the system has a calming effect on the organs,

Diagram labels

Left side (Sympathetic):
- Narrows pupil
- Stimulates secretion from salivary glands
- Slows heart
- Sugar in liver stored
- Movement of stomach accelerates
- Rectum contracts
- Bladder contracts

Right side (Parasympathetic):
- Widens pupil
- Suppresses secretion from salivary glands
- Accelerates heart
- Sugar from liver released
- Movement of stomach slowed
- Rectum relaxes
- Bladder relaxes

SYMPATHETIC

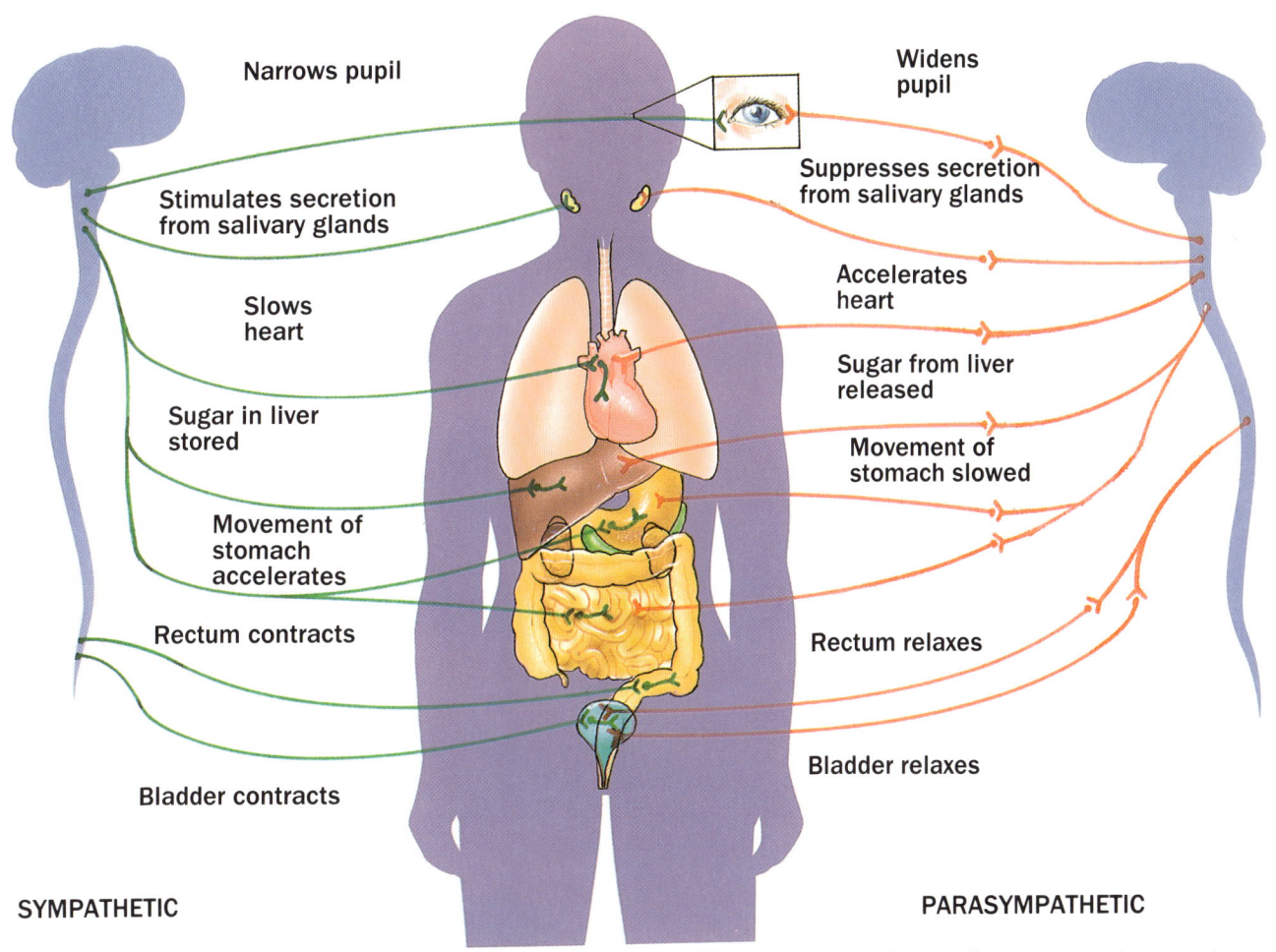

△ The autonomic nervous system works without conscious control to maintain the functions of the vital internal organs that keep us alive. The system is made up of two opposing parts. The sympathetic part of the system has a stimulating effect on the organs, causing them to increase their activity, whereas the parasympathetic part

PARASYMPATHETIC

relaxes the organs, decreasing their activity. The two systems balance each other, allowing for both exertion and rest, but preventing dangerous extremes of either.

slowing down their activity; the other speeds up their activity. For example, if we are suddenly angry or frightened by something, one half of the system acts very strongly. Blood is sent to muscles, heartbeat increases and the lungs breathe more deeply. Without knowing it, we are ready to fight or run away.

The endocrine system works alongside and in partnership with the autonomic nervous system. The endocrine system is made up of glands all over the body. They empty hormones — chemical messengers — directly into the bloodstream. Hormones also increase or decrease the activity of organs, which may be some distance away. The hormones reach the organs concerned within a minute.

△ Nerves and hormones both act in dangerous situations.

EXTRAORDINARY SENSES

Many animals have the same senses as humans, but often they are much more sensitive. Other animals have very different senses from our own. They are sensitive to things that we have only discovered through science. Many animals, such as whales and bats, use high-pitched sounds that they makes to "see" objects. Some animals, such as electric eels, are sensitive to electric currents. The blind salamander (below) lives in the complete darkness of caves, but it can easily find its way around. It can sense the Earth's magnetic field rather like a compass can.

Migrating birds

Many animals migrate long distances to follow sources of food and avoid bad weather. Some migrating birds travel distances as great as half way round the world or more. Their sense of direction rarely fails, even though young birds may not have made the journey before. Birds use magnetic clues, and more experienced birds also use the positions of stars, the Sun and landmarks as they approach their destination.

Blind salamander

Snakes have poor hearing and sight, but their senses of smell and taste are very good. They flick their tongues into the air, where they pick up molecules of scents. The tongue is drawn into the mouth and placed in a special sense organ in the roof of the mouth. Some snakes also have heat-sensitive pits on the sides of their faces or lips which can detect the infra-red heat rays given off by animals the snakes hunt as prey.

Star-nose mole

Touch is a very important sense to many animals. The star-nose mole lives in tunnels in the ground but it catches its food from the bottoms of streams. It can find small animals, such as insects and fish, by feeling with the sensitive finger-like projections on its nose. Moles are also very sensitive to the vibrations of the earth around their tunnels. Fish are sensitive to vibrations in the water around them. They can detect changes in pressure caused by the presence of other animals. The organs concerned are the lateral lines. These are canals that run along each side of a fish's body and contain receptor cells.

Heat sensitive pits

GLOSSARY

Autonomic nervous system
The part of the nervous system that controls organs of the body without us being aware of what is happening.

Axon
The part of a nerve fibre that carries signals away from the main part (the cell body) of a neurone.

Central nervous system
The brain and the spinal cord.

Dendrite
A small branching dendron that connects to another neurone.

Dendron
The part of a nerve fibre that carries signals towards the main part (the cell body) of a neurone.

Hormone
A chemical that is produced by glands in the body. Hormones (together with the autonomic nervous system) control the functions of organs of the body.

Membrane
A thin layer that covers a part of the body, such as the lining of the nose, or the outer living layer of a cell.

Nerve
A neurone or a bundle of neurones.

Nerve impulse
An electrical signal that travels along a neurone.

Neurone
A special type of cell that carries electrical signals in the body.

Organ
A part of an animal that has particular functions; for example, an eye is an organ that sees.

Perception
The process of getting information about the world by using the various sense organs.

Reasoning
Thinking that involves the conscious analysis of information; for example, doing a mathematical problem or analyzing the results of an experiment.

Reflex action
An automatic and uncontrollable reaction to a stimulus.

Sense
One of the ways in which an animal gets information about the world; for example, sight or touch.

Sense organ
Any organ of the body that gathers some form of information about the world and turns it into nerve impulses; for example, an ear gathers information in the form of sound.

Spinal cord
A large bundle of nerves that runs down from the brain through the tube formed by the bones of the spine.

Stimulus
Anything that causes a nerve impulse to start; for example, heat on the skin or light entering an eye.

Synapse
A place where signals pass from one neurone to another.

Unconscious
A word that describes something that happens in the body without us knowing that it is happening. For example, we are unconscious of the autonomic nervous system controlling our digestive processes.

INDEX

A
actin 16
autonomic nervous system 8, 9, 28, 29, 31
axons 6, 31

B
balance 17
brain stem 10, 11

C
central nervous system 8, 10, 31
cerebellum 10, 11
cerebral cortex 10-13
cerebrum 10, 11
ciliary muscles 18
cochlea 20, 21
colour vision 19
conjunctiva 18
cornea 18

D
dendrites 6, 31
dendrons 6, 31
dermis 26
digestion 25

E
ears 17, 20
EEG machine 10
emotions 13
endocrine system 29
epidermis 26, 27
extraordinary senses 30
eyes 17-19

G
grey matter 8, 10

H
hearing 20
heat 26, 27
hippocampus 14
hormones 9, 29, 31
hypothalmus 10, 13

I
information 7, 12-14
internal senses 28, 29
iris 18

L
learning 14, 15
limbic system 13

M
medulla 10, 11
Meissner's corpuscle 26
membranes 6, 7, 31
memory 14, 15, 22, 25
midbrain 10, 11
monitoring 28, 29
motor neurones 7-9, 16
movement 16, 17
muscles 16-18, 24, 27
myelin 6

N
nasal cavity 22
nerve cells 6, 7, 22
nervous system 5, 8, 9
neurones 6, 7, 12, 31
nodes of Ranvier 6
nose 22-25

O
olfactory organs 22, 23
optic nerve 18

optical illusions 13

R
pain 26
parasympathetic system 29
perception 12, 13, 31
perilymph 21
peripheral nervous system 8-9
pheromones 23
pituitary gland 10
pons 10, 11

R
reflex actions 9, 28, 31
retina 18, 19
rods and cones 18, 19

S
saliva 24, 25
Schwann cells 6
sensory nerves 8, 9, 18, 21, 26, 28
sight 18, 19
signals 6, 7, 12, 16, 20-22
skin 26, 27
smell 22-25
spinal cord 8, 9, 11, 16, 28, 31
sympathetic system 29
synapses 6, 7, 12, 16, 31

T
taste 24, 25
thalamus 10
tongue 24, 25
touch 26, 27

Photographic Credits:
Cover and pages 7, 10, 22 and 26: Science Photo Library; pages 5, 20 and 27 bottom: Bruce Coleman; pages 12, 13, 14 both, 15, 27 top and 28 bottom: Marie-Helene Bradley; page 21: Eye Ubiquitous; pages 23 top, 28 top and 30 centre left and right: Frank Lane Picture Agency; pages 23 bottom, 29, 30 top and bottom: Planet Earth Pictures; page 25: Spectrum Colour Library.